23 THINGS TO DO before you are 11½

QED

QED Publishing

Written by Mike Warren
Editor: Louisa Somerville
Managing Editor: Laura Knowles
Designer: Clare Barker/ Martin Taylor
Art Director: Susi Martin
Publisher: Zeta Jones
Associate Publisher: Maxime Boucknooghe
Production: Nikki Ingram

First published in the UK in 2014 by Marshall Editions

ISBN 978 1 78493 034 9

Originated in Hong Kong by Cypress Colours (HK) Ltd
Printed and bound in China
by 1010 Printing International Ltd

10 9 8 7 6 5 4 3 2 1   14 15 16 17 18

NOTE TO PARENTS

The projects in this book are of varying levels of difficulty, and many require the use of tools. They are designed to be constructed with adult help, and not for the child to make on his or her own.

Children should be supervised at all times when using potentially dangerous equipment.

The author and publisher accept no liability for any injuries sustained in making these projects, which are undertaken entirely at your own risk.

contents

projects

How to use this book

Using tools to make cool stuff is just for adults, right? Not necessarily! So long as you are careful, you can easily get started on these great projects.

With the right tools and knowledge, you can learn the skills to make these projects, and even begin to design your own.

It's important that an adult is present to help you with the tricky bits and to make sure that you are using the tools safely. Make sure that you show your parent, grandparent, or enthusiastic uncle or aunt which project you want to embark on, so that they can help you. It's much more fun to make things together, anyway!

All the projects in this book are colour coded into four categories:

SUPER SCIENTIST

The science behind each project is explained so that you will understand why the project works, as well as how.

WORKSHOP WIZARD

You'll need workshop tools and skills, such as sawing and a drilling, to complete these projects. You may need some adult help, too.

OUTDOOR ADVENTURER

These are practical projects for when you are out and about in the great outdoors. Perfect for when you're camping out or exploring.

ECO DUDE

These projects are designed to help you take care of your environment, and use lots of recycled materials.

REMEMBER: SAFETY FIRST!

- ALWAYS ask permission before starting a project
- NEVER use tools or knives without adult supervision
- ALWAYS follow safety instructions
- NEVER fool around with tools or knives

STEP-BY-STEP

Every project in this book has step-by-step instructions for you to follow. Read through the instructions before you begin, and then re-read each step carefully before you start it.

It's as easy as 1, 2, 3...

The secret to a successful project is proper preparation! That means getting all your materials and tools ready before you begin. At the beginning of every project, you'll see one of these boxes, telling you all the equipment and supplies you need.

you will need

- A4 sheets of card
- A4 sheets of paper
- clear plastic wallets or sealable bags
- pencil
- ruler
- scissors

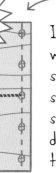

Take care!

It's important to tell a grown up what you plan to do, and have someone close by to help. Where you see these signs, it means that the step is particularly tricky or could be dangerous, so an adult should be there to give you a hand.

* * * * * *

* There are quick tips throughout the book – don't forget to read them!

* * * * * *

This type of box tells you extra information behind the project. Whether it's how a paper airplane flies, how to build a campfire, or what earthworms like to eat, you'll find it in these fact boxes.

LOOK OUT FOR THESE BOXES...

...you never know what interesting things you might find out to impress your friends!

You're nearly ready to begin...

How to use your tools safely

Every project-maker needs a good set of tools in their tool kit, but it's essential to learn how to use them safely.

TOOL BOX

Safety goggles

Safety goggles are a very important piece of kit. Always put them on before drilling or hammering to protect your eyes, in case any nails or splinters of wood go flying.

Drills

It can be handy to use power tools, such as drills, but they can be dangerous if not used correctly. **Never** use a drill without adult supervision.

DRILL

Take care!

First of all, put on your safety goggles. Make sure that loose clothing such as long sleeves won't get in the way, and if you have long hair, tie it back.

Ask an adult to help you put in the correct size drill bit and set the drill to the right setting. Make sure it is locked in tight. Together, you should practise drilling some holes in a spare piece of wood. That way, you'll be able to make neat holes in the right places when you come to make one of the projects.

Drill bits

A drill bit is the metal piece that fits in the end of the drill. The drill spins the bit very fast, to bore a hole in the wood. Drill bits come in various sizes, to make different sized holes.

Hole saw

This special drill attachment is like a drill bit, but it is used to cut out a larger hole in a piece of wood.

Saw

To cut through wood

WOOD SAW

with a saw, you move the saw backwards and forwards along the line you want to cut, pushing down slightly. It's best to practise on some spare wood, before you start making one of your projects. Don't forget to wear your safety goggles, and keep your fingers out of the way!

Hacksaw

HACKSAW

This is a fine-toothed saw that can be used on wood, and thin pieces of metal or plastic.

Hammer

A hammer is used to tap nails into wood. Start off with a few very gentle taps to get the nail positioned in the

HAMMER

wood, being very careful not to hit your fingers. Then take your fingers away, and tap the nail a little harder to push it right into the wood.

Clamp

A clamp is used to fix an object in place, to keep it steady while you are working on it. You can clamp a piece of wood to a workbench, so that it doesn't jiggle around while you are sawing it.

Vice

A vice is usually fixed to the top of a workbench. It has fixed and moveable jaws and is very useful for gripping things while you work.

Glue gun

A glue gun melts a stick of glue, and then pushes very hot glue out of a nozzle. When the glue cools, it hardens and is very strong. It can be used on wood, plastics, and card.

GLUE GUN

Take care to hold the glue gun correctly. Don't touch the hot glue, or you could get burnt. **Make sure an adult is there to check you are using it safely.**

Soldering iron

A soldering iron is an electric tool that melts a type of soft metal, called solder, that is used to join pieces of metal together. The solder and soldering iron get extremely hot, and **should be used under adult supervision.** If you don't have your own soldering iron, there might be one you could ask to use at your school.

Sanding block

A sanding block or sandpaper is used to smooth down the rough edges of wood. It's best to wear a face mask while sanding, so that you don't breathe in any dust.

Awl

This tool is used for making a small hole in a piece of wood, so that it is easier to put a drill bit, or screw in the right place, without damaging the wood. (The end of a nail makes a useful alternative.)

Screwdriver

This simple tool is an essential piece of kit. A cross-head screwdriver, also called a Phillips screwdriver, is used for screws with a cross on the top, and a flat-head screwdriver is used for ones with a single groove on the top.

Craft knife

Craft knives are very sharp, so you must be very careful when you use them, and never touch the blade. The blade can be retracted back into the handle for safety when the knife isn't being used. **Don't use a craft knife without an adult's permission.**

Pliers

Pliers are used for gripping small objects and bending wire. They're a very handy tool to keep in your toolbox.

PLIERS

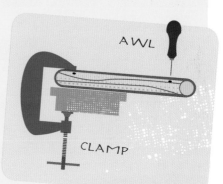

AWL

CLAMP

Everyday toolbox

you will need

- 6.4mm exterior grade plywood (x3) for base and sides, (cut to sizes shown)
- 12.5mm plywood (x2) for ends, as shown
- 6.4mm plywood for partition (x2), as shown
- 460mm x 25mm dia. wooden dowel
- drill and 3mm drill bit
- ruler and pencil
- set square
- 25mm hole saw
- screws and nails
- wood glue

Every good builder has a place to keep their tools, ready to be used for the next project. As a rite-of-passage, you should construct your own toolbox. If you take good care of it, it will last for a good many years!

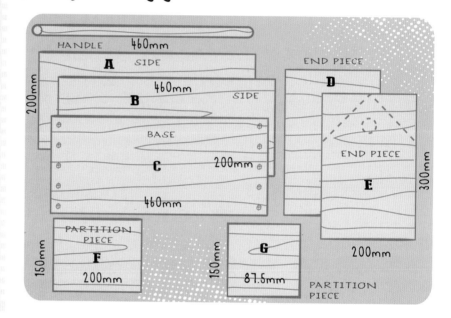

HANDLE   460mm
A   SIDE
200mm
B   460mm   SIDE
C   BASE   200mm
460mm
END PIECE
D
END PIECE
E   300mm
200mm
PARTITION PIECE
150mm   F   200mm
150mm   G   87.5mm
PARTITION PIECE

Take care!

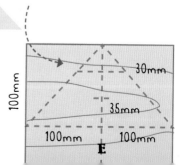

1. Starting with the base of the toolbox, put a 3mm drill bit into the drill. Now make 5 marks, equally spaced, about 6mm from both short edges, then drill the holes.

6mm

C

2. Next, using a ruler, measure down 100mm and draw a line across. Measure 100mm along the line, and using a set square then ruler, draw a vertical line to the full length.

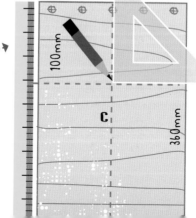

C   100mm   360mm

3. For the end pieces, measure 100mm along and draw a line. Now draw a vertical line 100mm along this line. Draw 2 more lines to make a point. Next, draw a line 30mm from the point, then make another mark 35mm further along.

100mm   30mm   35mm   100mm   100mm   E

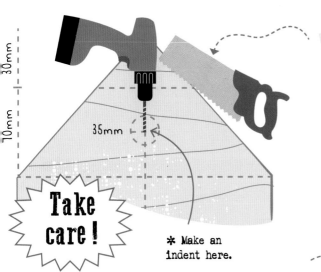

Take care!

* Make an indent here.

35mm

30mm

10mm

4. Carefully saw off the corners, then cut along the top straight line. With a nail or awl, make an indent into the 35mm mark, then insert the hole saw into the drill and make a 25mm hole, using the indent as a guide. Now shape and drill the other end piece in the same way. Finally sand all rough edges smooth with sandpaper.

5. Next, take one of the side panels, and make a series of holes 6mm from the ends. Measure along 100mm and draw a vertical line. Repeat for the other side panel.

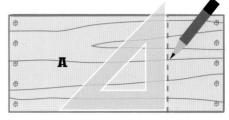

A

100mm

Assembling the toolbox

6. Add a line of glue along the bottom edge of the end pieces, then screw through the holes in the base into the bottom of the end pieces.

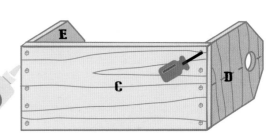

E

C

D

7. Next add a line of glue along the side edges of the end pieces, then screw the side panels in place, along the side pieces.

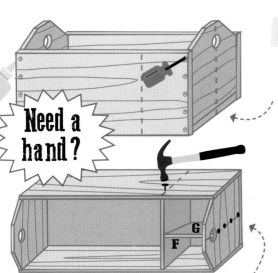

Need a hand?

F

G

8. Finally, put a line of glue along the side edges of the partition pieces, then nail the panels in place, through the side pieces along the lines you have drawn in Steps 2 and 5.

* Slide the dowel handle into the holes and use a little glue to hold in place.

9

Knots everybody needs to know!

A basic knowledge of knots can be really useful and could get you out of a tricky situation! Here are some basic knots to try...

Sheet bend

This is the best knot to use to tie two ropes together. This is a very sturdy knot, but beware: it can work loose when not under load!

1. Form a loop with rope A.

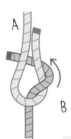

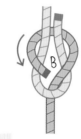

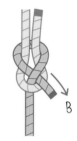

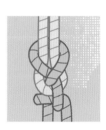

2. Pass rope B up through and round the back of rope A.

3. Bring B round to the front and pass behind the back of B.

4. Pull B tight to finish.

* For extra security loop the tail end of B back around rope B and feed through the loop.

Figure of eight

This is a great knot to stop the ends of your rope from pulling out of devices such as pulleys or a carabiner (a D-shaped metal loop). Historically used by sailors, it is now also used by mountain climbers.

1. Form a loop with the rope and twist twice.

2. Bring the end round to the front and pass down through the loop.

3. Pull tight to make the final knot.

Bowline

Used to form a fixed loop at the end of a rope, and since it's so easy to tie (and especially untie) it really is the king of knots. This knot tightens when under load.

sailors use bowline knots on board ship

  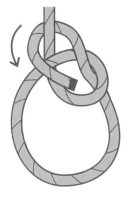 

1. With the rope form a small loop.

2. Pass the rope end up through the loop to form a larger loop.

3. Now take the rope around the back and bring it back down through the small loop.

4. Pull tight to finish.

Clove hitch

This rope is great for tying off to a post or tree. You can loosen the knot by feeding the rope in either direction, or use the quick release method.

* If a quick release is needed, double back the end of the rope under the second loop.

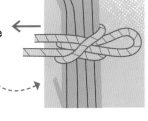

 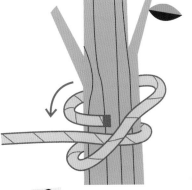 

1. Wrap the rope around the tree, then take it round the back a second time to form a second loop.

2. Now pass the end of the rope under the second loop.

3. Pull tight to secure the rope in place.

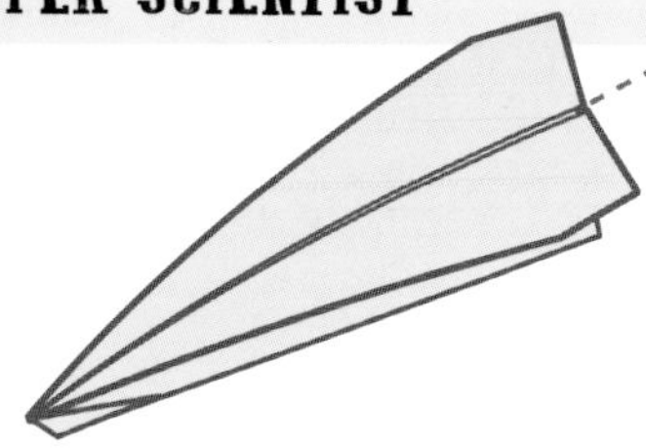

Ultimate paper aeroplane launcher

You can take paper plane flights higher and faster with an elastic launch system. All you need are basic office supplies.

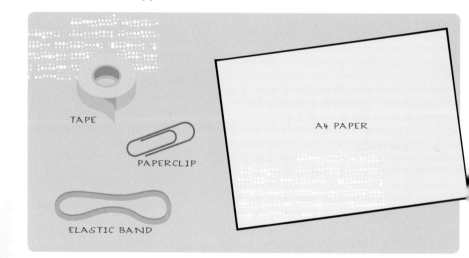

TAPE

PAPERCLIP

ELASTIC BAND

A4 PAPER

you will need

- A4 sheet of paper
- paperclip
- sticky tape
- elastic band

CAUTION: Launch your plane outdoors, and aim it away from people, pets, and breakable objects!

First make the aeroplane

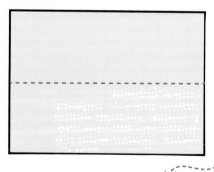

1. Fold the paper in half lengthways. This is called a valley fold (as it forms a valley shape).

2. Grab a corner and fold it back diagonally until the side edge is lined up with the valley fold to make a triangle. Flip the paper over and repeat on the other side.

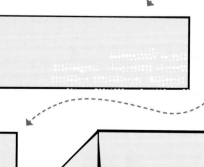

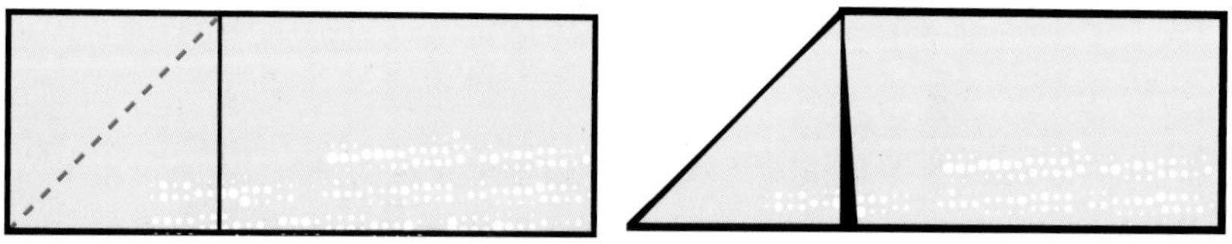

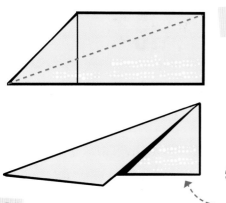

3. In the same way as before, fold down the folded section towards the valley fold again. Flip the sheet over and repeat on the other side.

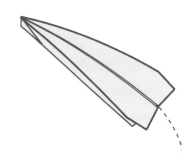

4. Once again, fold down towards the valley fold. Flip the sheet over and repeat on other side.

* Smooth the folds down with your fingertips to make them really sharp.

5. Ease the last folds you made upwards to make the plane's wings.

time for the test flight...

6. Next lay the plane down with the wings flat on the worksurface, and carefully unfold the wings.

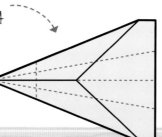

7. Fold the tip back into the valley fold.

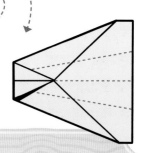

LIFT AND AEROFOILS

Aeroplanes fly by using a force called lift. As an airplane moves forwards, air flows over the wings, and lift pulls the plane upwards at the same time.

The streamlined shape of an aeroplane's wing is called an aerofoil. It is a curved shape, so that air flows faster over the wing and increases lift. A helicopter's rotor blades are also shaped liked aerofoils, to help it take off fast.

The opposite force to lift is drag, which acts to slow a plane down. (Learn about drag on p 42.)

Now for the tow hook

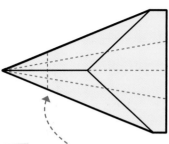
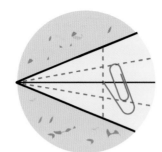
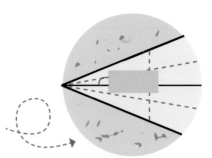

1. Lay the airplane flat again to reveal the nose fold you just made. You should now be able to see where the nose fold meets the valley fold.

2. Using the end of the bent paperclip, puncture a hole through the fold intersection. (There's only one layer of paper in this exact spot, so it's easy).

3. Push the end of the paperclip through the opening as far as the bend, then tape the paperclip onto the nose of the airplane.

4. Fold the nose back again. You should now just have the end of the paperclip sticking through the hole you made, with the rest tucked in underneath the nose fold.

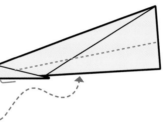

5. Continue folding the paper airplane wings back into shape.

Time for the launch

1. Stretch a rubber band over your thumb and index finger.

2. Feed the end of the tow hook through the rubber band.

watch it fly through the sky...

3. Grab the paper airplane where the paperclip lies, pull back until the rubber band is taut, then release!

Cool kite

you will need

- heavy-duty white or coloured bin bag, at least 110cm x 80cm
- 5mm diameter wooden dowels, at least 105cm long (x2)
- thin strips of craft dowel
- thick twine, 30m long
- string
- scissors
- marker pen
- metal tape measure
- ruler and set square
- hacksaw
- wide adhesive tape
- needle and thread
- glue gun

Making a kite is a classic project. When your kite is finished, all you need is a windy day! You can fly your kite in a garden or park - or better still, on a hilltop.

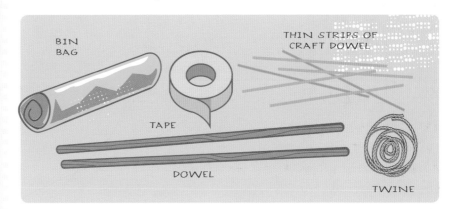

BIN BAG

THIN STRIPS OF CRAFT DOWEL

TAPE

DOWEL

TWINE

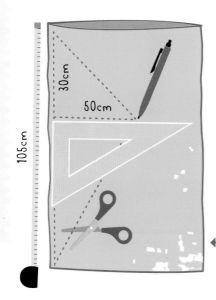

30cm

50cm

105cm

1. Cut the top 2cm off the bin bag, then pull out the pleated edges to make a flattened tube, and lay it on the floor. Now measure and mark 105cm along one long edge of the bag. Measure a further 30cm along the same edge and mark. This is the kite's centre point.

2. At the 30cm mark, use a set square to make a 50cm mark at a right angle. Draw lines to connect the marks to form a triangle. Cut out the triangle and unfold it flat on the floor. This is your basic kite shape.

15

3. Place a wooden dowel along the length of the kite and trim with a hacksaw to match the length of the kite. Tape over the dowel and around the bin bag, securing them all together at the top and the bottom.

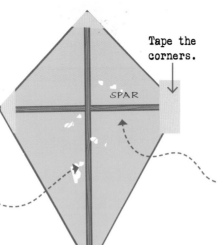

Tape the corners.

SPAR

4. Place second dowel at a right angle to the spine, at the centre point marked earlier, and trim as before. Tape in place on the other two corners of the bin bag, and secure with tape as before. (This cross-bar is called a spar.)

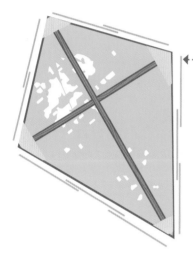

5. Place four pieces of thin craft dowel around the edges of the kite. If your dowel isn't long enough, you can use more pieces and overlap the ends by about 2.5cm.

6. To secure overlapped dowels, lash the ends together using a needle and thread. Add a dab of hot glue over each connection to secure it and hold the thread in place. Repeat for the other three sides.

7. Now place your pieces of dowel about 10mm inside the edge of the kite and lash them together where they cross-over at each corner. Carefully lift the dowel frame and put it to one side, then add a drop of glue to each crossover point.

8. Next place the dowel frame over the main kite structure and fold the edge of the plastic over the frame. Then tape securely in place, to make the kite really strong.

9. For extra strength, use the tip of a skewer to poke 2 small holes through the bin bag where the central dowels overlap. Feed the string through the holes and around the dowels a few times and tie off in a knot.

Need a hand?

Glue spot.

Make a winder

It's easy to make a winder. Simply place two lollypop sticks a handspan apart and apply glue at the spot marks shown. Cross with two more sticks, apply more glue, then a last layer of sticks, and leave to dry. Finally, trim with a hacksaw!

10. For the tail, measure and cut long, thin strips from the leftover bin bag. Tie 2 or more strips together to form a tail that's at least 2m long. Using more twine, bind the tail to the end of the kite and secure with more tape.

11. Measure and cut about 20m of twine. Knot one end to where the dowels cross in the centre of kite. (Use a bowline knot, see page 11.) The loose end of the twine is your kite's lead. The longer the lead, the higher your kite can fly.

watch your kite fly high...

Decoration

You could tie tissue paper bows onto the tail for decoration or stick a picture onto your kite with strong tape.

FLYING YOUR KITE

Choose a windy day! Stand with your back to the wind, and about 1m of slack in the kite line. Let the wind catch the kite and walk backwards, slowly releasing the slack. The kite should climb while you release the rest of the line.

TAKING CONTROL: Try attaching twine to the ends of the spars and then tie it off about 3m down the kite lead, to form a bridle for your kite. Flying may be harder at first, but you'll have more control.

17

Pop-bottle greenhouse

Almost all plants need a little help to get started. To grow big and strong, they need warmth and moisture. You can provide these conditions by making a windowsill pop-bottle greenhouse for your seeds.

you will need

- 2-litre clean, dry clear plastic pop bottle
- cardboard egg box (for 12 eggs)
- plastic bag
- compost (from your wormery see page 44)
- seeds
- marker pen
- knife
- scissors
- duct tape
- spoon
- small jug or cup
- water
- small plant pot (optional)

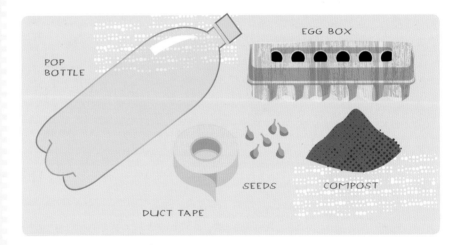

POP BOTTLE

EGG BOX

DUCT TAPE

SEEDS

COMPOST

1. Lie the bottle on its side and mark a line below the curve of the neck. Turn the bottle and continue the line around the whole bottle.

2. Carefully pierce the line with a sharp knife, then cut along it with the scissors.

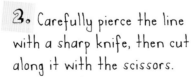

3. Join the top of the bottle (which you have just cut off) to the bottom with duct tape, to create a hinge. Now you can open and close the bottle.

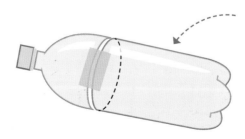

GROWING BEE-FRIENDLY PLANTS

Bees pollinate the plants in our gardens. Without bees, many fruit and vegetables would never get to the harvest stage, so it is a good idea to plant seeds that will grow into flowers that attract bees.

Here are some bee-friendly flowers that you can easily grow from seeds in your pop-bottle greenhouse:

- forget-me-not
- nasturtium
- cornflower
- catmint
- thyme
- lavender
- marigold
- hollyhock
- sage
- sunflower

4. Next cut the lid off the egg box, then trim the base so it will fit inside the pop bottle.

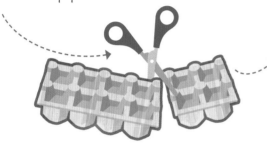

5. Put a seed in each egg box cell and spoon some compost over it.

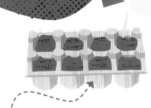

6. Now carefully water the compost.

7. Place the seeded egg box base inside the bottle and close the hinged end.

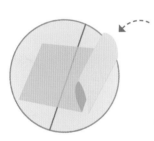

✻ You can make a tape catch by doubling up some tape for extra security.

8. Put the bottle on a windowsill indoors, in a sunny spot, for a week or so and watch your plants begin to sprout.

9. After about 2 weeks, when the seedlings sprout and are too big for your mini greenhouse, transfer them to a small pot or plant them in a garden and continue to watch them grow!

Treasure map trail

Treasure hunting is a fun way to spend the afternoon, and is a great way to test your friends' orienteering skills - while testing your ability to think up fiendishly clever clues!

you will need

- A4 sheets of card
- A4 sheets of paper
- clear plastic wallets or sealable bags
- pencil
- ruler
- scissors

Start by thinking of a good location to have your hunt. Choose somewhere that is large enough to challenge your treasure seekers, but not so large that they can get lost! Try your house on a rainy day, or a nearby park on a sunny day.

1. Draw a plan of the treasure hunt area. If it's outdoors, you may be able to print out an aerial view from the internet.

2. On the plan, mark the places where you will leave the clues and the treasure. Draw a dotted line to show the trail from clue to clue.

3. Now make up the clues. (See page 21 for ideas for clue writing.) They should be challenging, but not so hard that your friends can't solve them!

4. Write each clue on a separate sheet of paper and place each one in a clear plastic wallet to protect it from the elements.

❋ Tip: Show your clues to an adult to test that they aren't too easy or too hard!

5. Hide the clues (apart from the first one) and the treasure.

6. Gather your friends and give them the first clue. Time to begin! (Remember to try the hunt yourself first, making sure the hunt can be done and you have an idea how long it will take.) A good treasure hunt has challenging but fun puzzles, and enough clue locations to keep things interesting.

❋ This is your masterplan. Don't show it to anyone!

types of clues...

Here are some ideas for different types of clues:

Riddle

Question; What has holes all over, but holds water?

Answer: 'a sponge'. (Put next clue under a sponge in the bathroom.)

Anagram

Muddle up the letters of a clue.

HIBDEN ETH SORE HUBS

(BEHIND THE ROSE BUSH)

Rhymes

Replace some clue words with rhyming ones.

Cook on the burst elf of the midge.

(Look on the first shelf of the fridge.)

Team work

Leave an item which the hunters must collect at each clue point. For example, leave balloons, straws, bottle caps, and cartons in each clue location. At the end of the hunt, each person can make a Balloon Car Racer (see page 42). Leave enough items for everyone to collect to make their finished car.

Jigsaw

Paste a picture onto thin card. When dry, cut it up into jigsaw pieces - one for each clue. At each clue location leave a puzzle piece in the bag with the clue. Hunters will need to collect all the pieces to complete the puzzle. This is a good way of making sure that your treasure hunters have completed the trail!

GEOCACHING

Another variation of a treasure hunt is geocaching. A geocache is a container hidden somewhere and the only clue given is its location (in terms of longitude and latitude found on a geographical survey map), along with a few descriptive identifiers. Explorers then embark to find the hidden cache.

Your geocache container should be waterproof with a tight-fitting lid, and contain a log book for people to sign, and some small trinkets to trade with other hunters.

People can also leave clues in the log book to lead others to their own geocache.

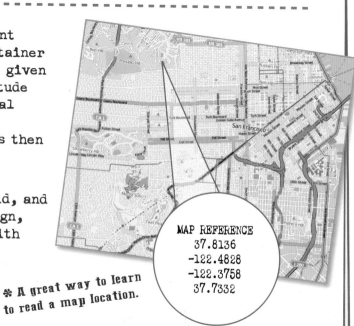

MAP REFERENCE
37.8136
-122.4828
-122.3758
37.7332

✳ A great way to learn to read a map location.

Ginormous bubbles

Regular bubbles are OK, but they're even better when they're bigger! Making your own giant bubbles is easy and fun. Because of the enormous size of these bubbles, and the mess they make when they burst, this project should be done outdoors.

you will need

- broom handles / large wood dowels / large sticks (x2)
- cotton or cloth rope / hemp rope
- large metal washer / nut
- eye bolts (x2)
- large bowl (x2)
- shallow bucket
- drill
- scissors

FOR THE BUBBLE MIX:

- 1 litre water
- 1 tbsp surgical spirit
- 1 tsp guar gum powder (found at supermarkets or online)
- 3 tbsp washing-up liquid

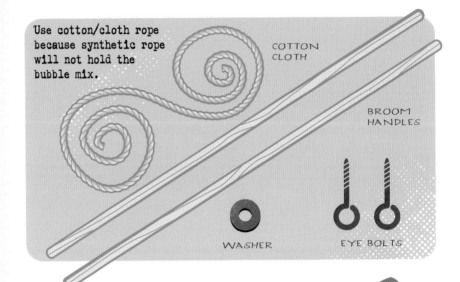

Use cotton/cloth rope because synthetic rope will not hold the bubble mix.

COTTON CLOTH

BROOM HANDLES

WASHER

EYE BOLTS

1. First, make a pair of bubble-maker wands. Drill a small hole into one end of each broom handle and screw in the eye bolts.

Take care!

2. Cut 2 metres of cloth rope with scissors and feed the washer or nut onto it, then tie the ends of the rope to the eye bolts.

The washer acts as a weight on the rope and helps to hold it in a U-shape.

3. Cut a 1-metre length of rope and tie this to the eye bolts as well. Your wands are ready.

let's get started

on the bubbles...

4. Pour the water into a large bowl, saving about a cupful in a separate bowl.

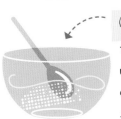

5. Add the surgical spirit to the cup of water in the second bowl, then slowly add the guar gum powder and mix to form a thin paste. (If you add the powder too fast, the mixture will go lumpy.)

6. Add the mixture to the water in the other large bowl, add the washing-up liquid and gently mix until completely combined. Pour into a shallow bucket and you're ready to go!

7. Holding the wands together, dip the ropes into the bucket and slowly pull out. With your back to the wind, slowly pull the wands apart to create a bubble film. Let it inflate with air and watch your giant bubble float away.

HOW A BUBBLE WORKS

Water is made up of molecules, and they like to stick together. Try slowly filling a cup of water to the brim (over a sink!). The water rises above the lip of the glass slightly before spilling over. It looks as if the surface of the water was coated with a stretchy elastic. The 'stickiness' of the water is called surface tension and is caused by the molecules as they interact with air.

Adding bubble mix to the water increases surface tension, allowing the liquid to stretch and make giant bubbles.

Further experiments
Customize your bubble maker by tying more rope inside the loop to form a web, which will create hundreds of smaller bubbles at once.

Super duper solar viewer

It's dangerous to look directly at the sun, so how can you find out what's going on up there? Make a solar viewer to see all the amazing things happening - without hurting your eyes.

you will need

- A4 sheet of thin card
- A4 sheet of thin paper
- cocktail stick or needle
- big, long cardboard box (such as a cardboard shipping box or shoe box)
- white paper
- pencil
- ruler
- set square
- scissors
- tinfoil
- tape

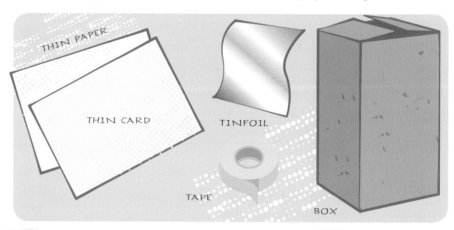

1. Fold a sheet of thin paper in half and in half again. Open it out and place it over the thin card. Push the point of a pencil through the centre of the paper to mark the centre point on the card below.

2. Using a pencil and set square, measure and draw two 10cm lines at right angles through the centre point.

3. Now draw 4 more 10cm lines to form a square and cut it out.

4. Cut a 15cm x 15cm square of tinfoil and tape it over the hole in the card. Poke a tiny hole (less than 1mm) in the centre with the cocktail stick or needle.

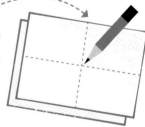

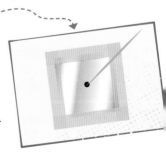

24

Very important!!

NEVER look directly at the sun, and NEVER look at it through binoculars.

5. On a sunny day hold the viewer in your hand and project the sun onto a white wall or sheet of paper on the ground. The further away the solar viewer is from the projection surface the larger the sun image will be. Take turns with a friend to hold the solar viewer while they check out the projected image.

project the sun onto a large sheet of paper

Super duper box viewer

1. Depending on your box size, cut a hole at one end of the box (leaving a supporting edge) and firmly tape the solar viewer over the centre of the hole. If the box end is smaller than the viewer card, cut the end off the box and trim the viewer to fit, taping all around the edges.

2. Next, cut an opening on the side of the box at the opposite end from the viewer. It will need to be at least 15mm high. Measure and trim a sheet of white paper to fit the end of the box.

supporting edge

✲ The box blocks reflected light from outside, so you can see more solar details, such as sunspots.

HOW THE VIEWER WORKS

This simple but effective method of viewing the sun is actually a type of 'camera obscura', the very first type of camera invented. It works the same way as a human eye. The light rays from the sun (or light rays reflected from any other object) travel through the tiny hole, which focuses them like a lens. As they travel through the hole, they are flipped over, projecting an upside-down image of the original object onto the paper.

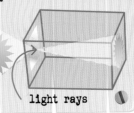

light rays

you will need

- 500ml wide-mouthed, plastic liquid container. With some neat packing you can fit all of the items listed below safely inside. This will keep all your emergency items in one place - and waterproof!

Emergency camping gear

If you are going to be out and about exploring for any length of time, it's important to make sure you have the right gear with you. Apart from dressing sensibly for the outdoors, there are some essential items every explorer should carry...

Pure wool socks

Wool doesn't retain water, making it ideal for keeping your toes warm.

Needle and thread

To repair any number of things when camping.

Bin bags

Large, waterproof, easy to pack, and endlessly customizable. There's no end to the usefulness of bin bags when camping. Here are a few ideas to get you started:

- Stuff a bin bag with clothes and tie tightly to make a seat to protect you from wet surfaces.

- Use one as a make-shift tarpaulin.

- With a hole in the bottom, it turns into a stylish rain poncho!

Whistle

To alert people to where you are, and scare away animals.

Thermal blanket

(moon blanket) One surface reflective, the other insulated.

First aid kit

You should have a basic first aid kit containing: bandages • iodine (disinfectant) • sling • tweezers • tensor bandage • antibiotic ointment • gauze

Water purification tablets

You might need these if you are going to be in remote areas without access to clean water.

Make a paracord bracelet:

1. Take a strand of paracord 5 times longer than your wrist's circumference. Secure the centre of the strand to a key loop. On one strand from the anchor, double up the paracord and wrap it around your wrist. (Two strands go around your wrist, through the loop.) Tie off the measured wrist length to the key loop.

2. Loop left strand with tail towards right side, over central strands. Repeat on right, going under strands. Place tails through loops on opposite sides.

3. Pull the tails tight. You just made the first weave of the bracelet.

4. Repeat the loops with one over the double strand in the middle and one under. To make it neat, keep all the over tails coming from the same direction.

5. Pull the tails through the loops tight and move onto the next weave.

6. Stop when you get near to the end of your double strand, to leave enough room for your key loop to fit into and secure the connection around your wrist.

7. Loop left and right segments. Pass tail through the double stranded middle and back. Pull tail to close loop.

Multi-tool
With knife blade, saw, pliers, and a tin opener.

5-10m paracord
Useful for knots and many other things.

Firelighters
(See firelighter project on page 32.)

Small mirror
Can be used to reflect sunlight to send a signal from far away.

Emergency rations
Shop-bought energy bars can be stored for a long time.

Rope ladder

Need a quick getaway to your favourite hideaway? Or want to get up to the top bunkbed to escape from your pesky brother or sister? Here's the answer - make your own rope ladder!

you will need

- wooden dowel / scrap lumber / 2x4 cut to 60cm lengths (for ladder rungs)
- high tensile rope (see note below)
- measuring tape
- pencil
- clamp
- nail or awl
- drill
- hole-cutting drill bit (one size larger than the diameter of the rope you will use)

Weigh-in

Make sure that the rope you use for your ladder is strong enough to bear your weight. If in doubt, weigh yourself and then check with your local hardware store.

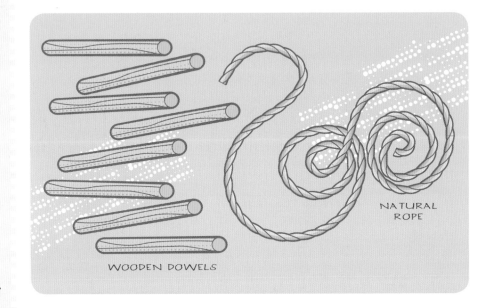

WOODEN DOWELS

NATURAL ROPE

1. Measure the height you want your ladder to reach, then add another ½ of the height to the overall height. (This allows extra rope for the knots end securing points.) Then double that length - as there's a rope on each side of the ladder.

2. Now decide how many rungs you will need. Divide the height of the ladder by about 20cm (or the distance you think you will need between each rung) and that will give you the number of rungs you need for your ladder.

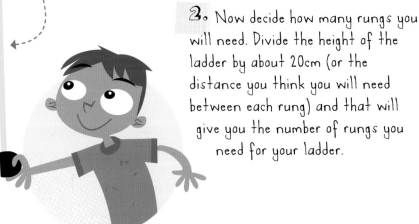

3. Take your first rung and measure in about 5cm from the end. Mark a dot where you are going to drill a hole for the rope. Repeat at the other end, then do the same for the rest of the rungs.

4. Hold or clamp one of the ladder rungs steady. Use a nail or awl to make an indent in the wood on top of your marks.

Take care!

5. Next, with the drill and drill bit, make a hole using the indent as a guide. Repeat for the other end, and for the rest of the rungs.

time to get knotting...

6. Starting from bottom of ladder, tie a knot on one end of each rope, then feed a ladder rung down the rope until it reaches the knot you just tied. Now tie another knot on the top side of the rung.

7. Measure up about 20cm and tie another knot in the rope, then feed another rung onto the rope. Repeat until you finish your ladder length. Do the same for the other side, matching the knot locations for level rungs.

TIP: Tie the ropes off into a top knot.

Build a bird nesting box

Build the perfect home for these tiny feathered friends. Little birds can be hard to spot but their songs will tell you they are around and happy to have a brand new home!

you will need

- 12.5mm hardwood (cut to sizes shown)
- 4cm piece of 6mm dowel
- ruler
- sanding block
- drill
- drill bits (3mm, and 6mm)
- 25mm hole cutter
- screwdriver
- paint (see page 31)
- paintbrush
- picture hooks or eyelets
- 20 alloy (non-rusting) screws

Giving nature a helping hand

Making a nesting box povides a safe home for birds to make a nest and raise their chicks. If put up in autumn, the box will also provide a winter roosting site for small species, such as the blue tit, wren, and house sparrow.

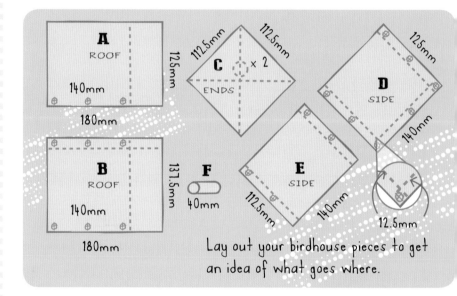

A ROOF — 140mm × 180mm

C ENDS × 2 — 112.5mm / 112.5mm / 125mm

D SIDE — 125mm / 140mm

B ROOF — 140mm × 180mm — 137.5mm

F — 40mm

E SIDE — 112.5mm / 140mm — 12.5mm

Lay out your birdhouse pieces to get an idea of what goes where.

1. First, sand off any rough edges from your pieces so they will sit flush to the other wood pieces. Wipe them with a damp cloth to remove any dust.

Take care !

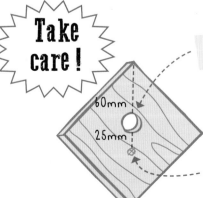

60mm
25mm

2. With a 25mm hole cutter make a hole in one of the C pieces, 60mm from the top. Sand the hole smooth. This opening will be the entrance to the bird box. Next make a mark 25mm below the entrance hole.

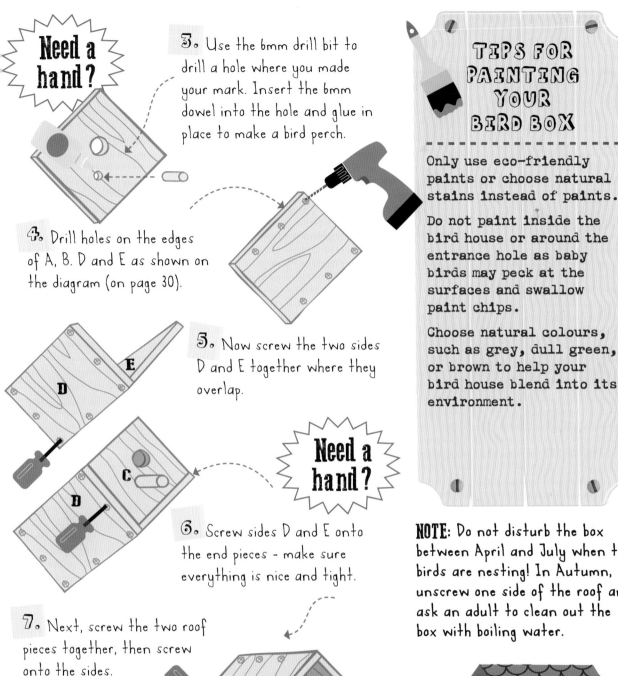

Need a hand?

3. Use the 6mm drill bit to drill a hole where you made your mark. Insert the 6mm dowel into the hole and glue in place to make a bird perch.

4. Drill holes on the edges of A, B. D and E as shown on the diagram (on page 30).

5. Now screw the two sides D and E together where they overlap.

Need a hand?

6. Screw sides D and E onto the end pieces - make sure everything is nice and tight.

7. Next, screw the two roof pieces together, then screw onto the sides.

You can now paint your birdbox. Depending on the type of paint, you might have to do 2 coats.

8. Finally, fix eyelets into the roof to hang the box, or picture hooks onto the back to nail it to a post or tree.

TIPS FOR PAINTING YOUR BIRD BOX

Only use eco-friendly paints or choose natural stains instead of paints.

Do not paint inside the bird house or around the entrance hole as baby birds may peck at the surfaces and swallow paint chips.

Choose natural colours, such as grey, dull green, or brown to help your bird house blend into its environment.

NOTE: Do not disturb the box between April and July when the birds are nesting! In Autumn, unscrew one side of the roof and ask an adult to clean out the box with boiling water.

Campfire firelighters

you will need

- old newspaper
- lint (gathered from a tumble-dryer filter, see page 63)
- string
- candle
- matches
- waterproof bag

It can be tricky getting a campfire started. That's why it's a good idea to come prepared with your own firelighter bundles. These easy-to-make firelighters will ensure a hot burn to get your fire going right first time.

DAILY NEW

LINT

STRING

WAX CANDLE

NEWSPAPER

1. Tear a page from an old newspaper into quarters.

2. Crumple the pieces and flatten them out again.

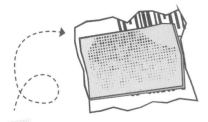

4. Loosely roll them together, then tie with string so it doesn't unravel. Repeat with the other pieces of newspaper.

3. Next place a generous amount of lint on a newspaper quarter.

Tip: Protect the work surface with more newspaper. Wax is tricky to remove from some surfaces.

Take care!

5. Lay the newspaper bundles on a work surface. Light the candle and drip wax all over the bundles.

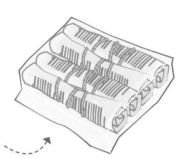

❋ Turn the bundles carefully, keeping your fingers well clear of the hot wax.

6. Once the bundles are coated with wax, leave until completely dry and stiff.

7. Pack your firelighters and matches into a waterproof bag until ready to use.

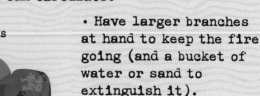

HOW TO BUILD A PERFECT CAMPFIRE

• Find a suitable location in a wide open area, with no overhead tree branches.

• Clear a space on flat, dry ground and use medium to large rocks to create a ring about a metre in diameter.

• Place a few firelighters in the centre of the firepit.

• Pile small, dry twigs and branches on top to form a loose pyramid, with lots of air gaps in the pile so that air can circulate.

• Have larger branches at hand to keep the fire going (and a bucket of water or sand to extinguish it).

• Light the firelighters. Your fire should catch immediately!

firelighters   rocks

twigs

Water log sword

Every swashbuckler needs a weapon to defend his or her territory! You can make your own foam sword with a water log (foam float) and a small length of dowel.

you will need

- water log
- broom handle / wooden dowel
- ruler / tape measure
- pen
- saw
- sandpaper
- PVC glue
- piece of cardbard
- scissors
- tape

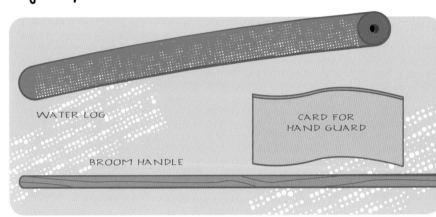

WATER LOG

CARD FOR HAND GUARD

BROOM HANDLE

Most water logs have a round cavity inside that is the perfect size to fit a broom handle. If you can't find an old broom handle (or toilet plunger handle), use a wooden dowel about the same size as your water log opening.

1. Measure 30cm in from the end of the water log and make a mark. Now measure the distance from the mark to the other end of the log and write it down.

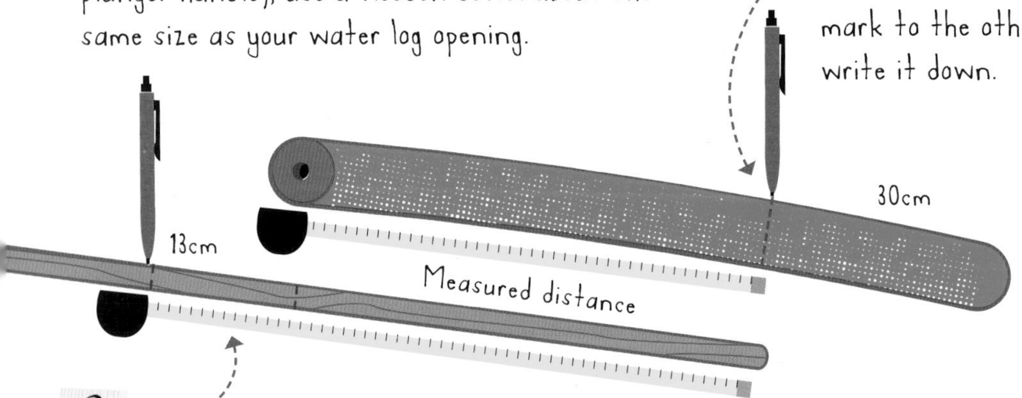

30cm

13cm

Measured distance

2. Now measure this distance along the dowel and make a line. Next add 13cm for the handle and make another line.

3. Hold the dowel and firmly saw through it at the second line.

Take care!

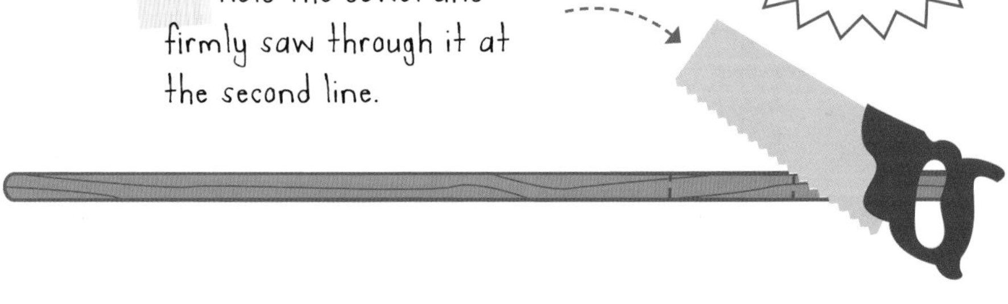

34

4. Round off the ends of the dowel with sandpaper. This prevents sharp edges from hurting yourself or others.

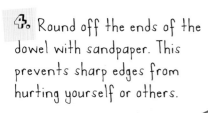

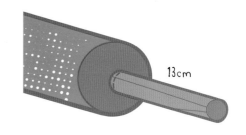

13cm

5. Holding the log at a slight angle, dribble some glue into the hole. (Not too much: you don't want it to drip through to the other end!)

6. Now slowly insert the handle into the end of the log up to the handle line. It should fit snuggly.

now for the hand guard

7. Cut a 125cm x 10cm rectangle from cardboard. (You can round off the corners if you like.) Gently bend the cardboard to arc around your fist.

8. Cut two circles roughly the diameter of the sword handle about 2.5cm from each end of the rectangle.

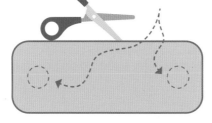

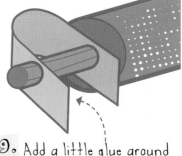

✻ Note the sword is bendy at the end so that it is safe to play with.

9. Add a little glue around the end of the water log, then slide the guard onto the handle, until it reaches the end. Add a bit of tape to hold the guard in place until it dries. That's it: you now have your own personal duelling weapon!

Taking it further
Experiment with the design to make short swords, or even a double-ended weapon!

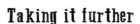

Make a pair of super stilts

Just can't wait to grow taller? Now you can, with stilts! Stilts are a classic carpentry project with a lofty pay-off. The great thing is that you can make stilts from things that you can easily find at your local hardware store.

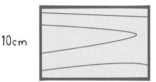

120cm

RISER PIECE

10cm

15cm

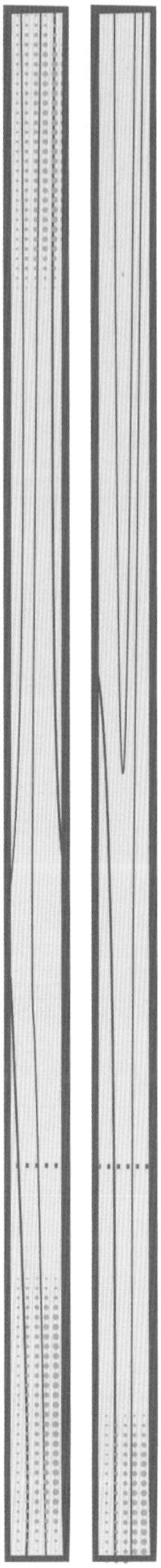

UPRIGHTS

you will need

- 120cm lengths of 5x5cm timber (x2)
- 15cm length of 5x10cm timber
- ruler and pencil
- set square
- hand saw
- power drill
- hole-cutting drill bit
- smaller drill bit
- very long screws (7cm and 10cm)
- wood glue

Centre of the riser

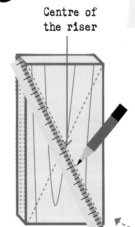

1. Lay the riser flat on a table and draw a line from one corner to the opposite corner. Draw another line to join the other two corners. Where the lines cross, make an X to mark the centre of the riser.

2. Place your set square so that the vertical edge is aligned with the edge of the wood and the hypotenuse (longest side) crosses the centre mark. Draw a line along the hypotenuse, to give a 45-degree angle.

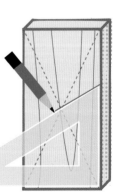

3. Use a hand saw to cut the wood along the pencil line. Now you have two halves of wood, each with a sloped side. These two halves will be your stilts' risers that you will stand on.

❋ Always check your measurements before cutting along the line!

Cut here

4. Now for the uprights! Decide how far up your uprights you'd like to stand. (Best not to make it too high, otherwise you might not have anything to hold onto!) Measure this distance from the end of the upright and mark the same level on the other upright.

TIP: Sand the uprights to avoid splinters

Take care!

5. Lay a riser on its long edge and mark an indent with an awl, then drill a hole slightly larger than the head of the screw. Drill for about 2.5cm. Finish the hole by drilling the rest of the way through with a bit slightly smaller than the size of the screw. Drill a similar hole into the sloping edge of the riser. Repeat for the other riser.

❋ A vice would be handy here to keep the block upright.

TIP: Add wood glue for extra strength.

6. Position the risers on the uprights, lining them up with your pencil marks. Screw into place. Then off you go!

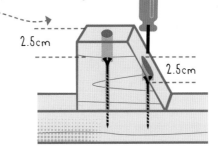

2.5cm

2.5cm

Further ideas
For a more comfortable handhold, you could bind the place where you grip the uprights with gaffer tape.

Buzzing robot bug

Ever wanted to have your own pet robot? In this project you'll use a simple electric circuit to make a vibrating robot 'bug'. Then you can have fun personalising your robot.

you will need

- coin cell battery and holder
- mobile phone vibration motor (harvested from an old mobile phone or available from electronics supply stores)
- 'helping hands' clamp tool
- soldering iron
- old toothbrush
- mug of hot water
- pliers
- glue gun
- tweezers
- pair of plastic joggle eyes
- paperclips (x2)

Note to parents

This project involves soldering together electrical components. Your child will need adult supervision as soldering irons are very hot. Take extra care when soldering, and work in a well-ventilated area.

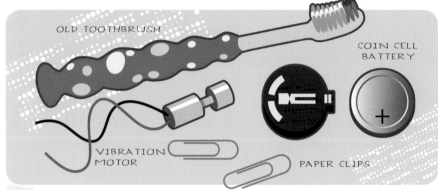

OLD TOOTHBRUSH

COIN CELL BATTERY

VIBRATION MOTOR

PAPER CLIPS

1. Clamp the empty battery holder and vibration motor close to each other in the 'helping hands'.

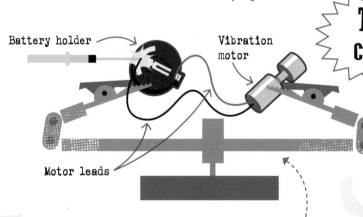

Battery holder

Vibration motor

Motor leads

Take care!

2. Carefully solder the motor leads to the battery holder to make a circuit. Test the circuit by putting the battery into the holder. The motor should vibrate.

3. Next, put the toothbrush in hot water to soak for a few minutes. Remove and gently press the bristles onto a surface to spread them out. Hold like this until they have cooled. Splayed bristles will better support your robot bug.

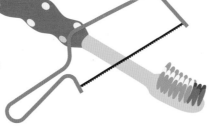

4. Now use the hacksaw to saw the head off the toothbrush, leaving about 2.5cm of handle for a tail.

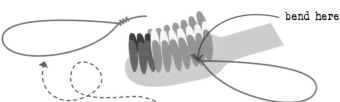

bend here

5. With a pair of pliers, open out and bend the paperclips into wing shapes. Twist the ends together and bend slightly. Put to one side.

PROVIDING THE POWER

Providing electrical current to the motor makes it spin. Be sure to provide the right amount of electrical power (3 volts), otherwise you might burn out your motor. Cell phone vibration motors are usually 3 volts, and most coin-cell batteries are also 3 volts.

time to make the bug...

6. Grip the bristles of the brush with the pliers to hold it firm, hold it face down and squirt a line of hot glue along the centre of the brush.

※ The motor's spindle must not touch the handle.

7. Holding the brush tightly, use tweezers to place the battery holder and motor on the brush. Leave to cool.

Make sure the battery holder and motor are exactly in the centre of the brush, so that they balance.

You may need help to glue the wings in place!

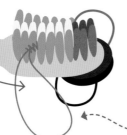

Take care!

8. Next, flip the brush over and insert the wings between the bristles. Fix in place with a spot of glue. Finally, glue the eyes to the front of the battery holder.

buzzzzzzzzzzzzzzzzzzz

9. Clip in the battery, set your robot bug on a flat surface and watch it go!

Secret booksafe

you will need

- hardcover book*
- plastic bag or clingfilm
- hard plastic sheet/ lid about the size of the book (to act as a cutting board)
- masking tape
- metal ruler
- bench vice / locking clamps
- sharp craft knife
- white glue
- 2.5cm paint brush

* NEVER destroy a good book! Buy an old one from a secondhand shop or ask an adult if they have one to spare. You could decorate the cover if you want to change the look of the book.

Make your own secret hiding place from an old hardcover book. By carving out the inside of a book, you can make a place to stash small personal items. Put the book on your bookshelf and hide your goodies where no one will find them...in full view!

MASKING TAPE   GLUE

PAINT BRUSH

BOOK

To make this book look untouched at a passing glance, you're only going to carve out the middle pages.

1. Gather about 10 pages in from the front of the book and wrap them, and the cover, in a small plastic bag (or clingfilm). Stick firmly with masking tape.

2. Count 10 pages from the back and slide the plastic sheet in front of them. Use four strips of masking tape to make a squared-off section around the new 'first' page at the front of the book.

Note to parents

This project uses a sharp knife. It is easily manageable for a child, but should definitely have adult supervision.

3. Now place a metal rule over the masking tape closest to the book spine, and use two clamps to secure the book and ruler to the edge of the work surface, making sure that the book cannot slip.

Take care!

❋ You may need help to secure the clamps.

Take care!

Hold the knife firmly and keep your fingers well out of the way!

❋ Cut from here to here.

4. Working slowly and carefully, use a craft knife to cut into the pages of the book along the metal rule next to the inside edges of the masking tape.

❋ Cutting through a book is hard work, so take a break if you're getting tired!

5. Start cutting at the corners to keep things neat. Cut through the paper until you reach the plastic sheet then stop. Rotate the book in the vice as you go, clamping it tightly each time.

6. After you have cut all the pages, unclamp the vice and remove any debris from the cutting area.

7. Pour some white glue into a pot then open up the back of the book. Remove the plastic lid, and use the brush to apply glue to the edge of the last cut page. Close the book.

8. Next, open the front of the book and carefully brush glue between all of the cut pages. Close the book and clamp tightly, leaving it to dry overnight.

9. Once the glue has dried, peel open the book and remove the masking tape and front cover plastic. Now you are ready to store your favourite goodies!

Vroom balloon racer

Hey, what's in the recycle box? Soft drink bottles, juice cartons? Transform these everyday items (washed, of course) into a super-fast racer. Get your friends to make their own... and start racing!

you will need

- rectangular, clean, dry juice carton
- straws (x2)
- large plastic bottle tops (x4)
- balloon
- ruler and pen
- scissors
- drill and drill bit
- stapler

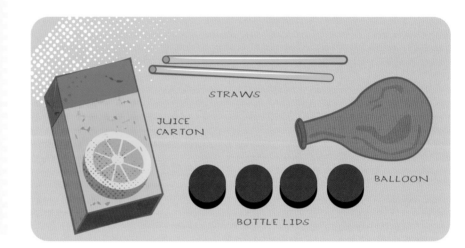

STRAWS

JUICE CARTON

BALLOON

BOTTLE LIDS

1. On one side panel of a juice carton, measure in about 2.5cm and mark a dot. Do the same at the other end of the panel. Now repeat on the other side panel of the carton.

2. With the point of the scissors, pierce the panel on the dot and twist to make a hole a bit bigger than the diameter of your straws.

Need a hand?

3. Use the scissors to cut off the front face of the carton. The open carton will be your racer's chassis.

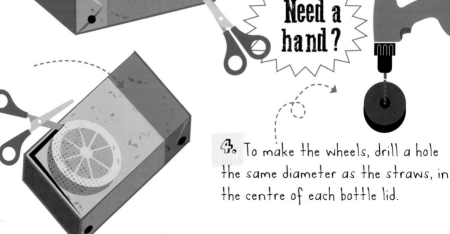

4. To make the wheels, drill a hole the same diameter as the straws, in the centre of each bottle lid.

AERODYNAMICS AND DRAG

Aerodynamics is the study of air as it moves around objects. Drag is a force that slows things down.

A racing car and an airplane have a pointed front, a flat underside, and a rear spoiler. This shape reduces drag by allowing air to pass swiftly over the car or plane,

and it therefore travels faster. You can use aerodynamics to improve the speed of your balloon racer by designing a wedge-like front for it like a racing car, and maybe a spoiler on the back. Can you think of other ways to make your racer have less drag?

5. Slide the straws through the chassis holes. Make sure they can rotate freely, and make the holes a bit bigger if they don't.

Tip: you can bend the end over to make it wider

6. Now slide a bottle lid onto each straw at both ends. Staple the straw to stop the wheels from coming off, then trim off any excess straw.

7. Pierce, then snip a hole in one end of the chassis for the balloon 'exhaust'. The exhaust hole must be large enough to let air escape from the balloon, but still hold the end of the balloon in place.

8. Place the balloon inside the box and feed the end through the hole. Inflate the balloon and pinch the neck. Put the car on a flat surface with the 'exhaust' facing you, and let go!

vroooooooom...

43

Make a wormery for compost

Making your own wormery for compost is as easy as drilling holes in a box! Any large plastic container with a lid will do, such as a laundry detergent tub or a stacking storage bin. Just add worms!

you will need

- 20-litre plastic container with lid
- drill and 2mm bit
- scissors
- weed barrier cloth (or cheesecloth)
- bucket
- paper
- soil
- food scraps (such as fruit and vegetable peelings, stale bread)
- bricks
- about 50 worms (from gardens, bait shops, or online suppliers)

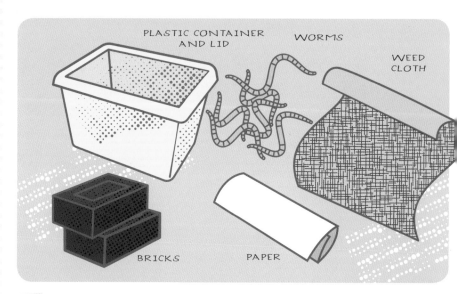

PLASTIC CONTAINER AND LID

WORMS

WEED CLOTH

BRICKS

PAPER

1. Drill some small holes in the bottom of the plastic container, for drainage.

you will need help to hold the container...

2. Drill more holes around the sides and lid of the container, for ventilation.

Take care!

3. Place the weed cloth over the bottom of the container and trim to fit the inside. Now put the cloth inside the container to stop soil from falling through the holes!

4. Next, shred your paper and pile it into a bucket. Add a little water to dampen it.

5. Fill the container ⅓ full with soil, then add a few worms along with some food scraps.

6. Now add a layer of the wet paper to the soil layer.

7. Continue layering soil, scraps, worms, and paper until the container is almost full. Don't press the soil down, as the soil needs air for the worms to make compost.

8. Now place the filled container on a few bricks, so that it drains properly, and cover it with a lid.

9. Your wormery is complete! Gradually add more food scraps, depending on how many worms you have and the size of the scraps.

your worms are alive so keep your wormery in a shady place...

WORMS: THE GARDENER'S FRIEND

Worms love to eat all kinds of food, especially food scraps, but not meat or dairy products because these may cause unpleasant smells or attract unwanted 'guests' into your worm bin.

Don't overdo one type of food, avoid bones or shells, and also very acidic things, like citrus peel.

Your worms will turn your waste into nutrient-rich compost (known as worm castings). These castings make a great fertilizer for all types of plants. They are the richest form of natural fertilizer.

Hardworking worms?
It should take the worms a month or two to make some nutritious compost, which you can use as fertilizer for your garden.
You could make a second wormery and rotate it with the first one after a few months, so that you always have a supply of compost. Throw the compost from the first wormery on your garden, saving the worms for your second wormery.

45

Stomp rocket launcher

Grab your space helmet: it's time to launch some rockets. Did you know you can make paper rockets that shoot up to 30 metres? Because of their speed, launch your rockets outside!

you will need

- 2m x 25mm diameter PVC pipe
- 25mm non-threaded coupler
- 25mm 4-way connector
- 25mm 45° PVC elbow
- end caps (x2)
- 2-litre pop bottle nd cap
- ruler
- marker pen
- saw
- drill and 12mm bit
- PVC glue
- A4 paper
- clear tape
- scissors
- face mask

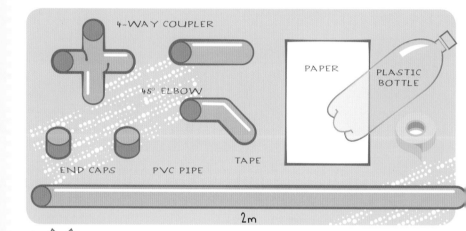

4-WAY COUPLER

45° ELBOW

PAPER

PLASTIC BOTTLE

END CAPS   PVC PIPE   TAPE

2m

Take care!

A   B   C

150mm   150mm   150mm

D

400mm

E

400mm

1. Measure along the 2m pipe and make a mark for 5 lengths: 150mm (x3) and 400mm (x2). Put on your face mask to avoid breathing in plastic dust. Hold the pipe firmly and saw it into the 5 sections, keeping the saw as straight as possible.

2. Take the 4-way connector and push pipes A and B into two of the opposite tubes, then add 2 end caps. This completes the stabiliser for your launcher.

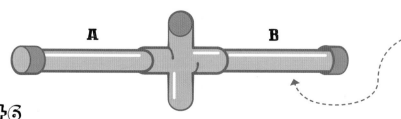

A   B

3. Next add pipe D to the stabiliser and pipe C to the opposite side. Attach the elbow pipe to pipe C, so that it points up at an angle towards you.

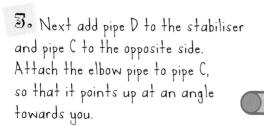

A

D

C

B

✳ don't glue here

4. Drill a hole in the centre of the bottle cap. Glue the cap into the end of pipe D. It should fit snuggly inside with the threads facing outwards. Don't glue over the hole.

Take care!

D

now take it apart again...

5. Check all fittings and if you are happy that everything is a nice snug fit, remove each component one at a time, add PVC glue to the coupler grooves and screw back together. (Don't glue the last 400mm pipe at the 45° elbow.)

Make the paper rocket

✳ make sure the tape is nice and flat

E

6. Wrap a sheet of paper around pipe E, just tight enough so that it can move along the pipe, and stick along the paper's edge with tape. Don't tape the pipe!

8. Now make the rocket fins. Cut a sheet of paper into a square, then fold into a triangle and tape along one of the edges. Make a 10mm fold along the other edge and snip off the point. Repeat to make 2 more fins.

7. Next, cut a disk of paper to cover the end of the pipe. Then slide the tube of paper to the top of the pipe, cover with the paper disk, and criss-cross over the end with pieces of tape, to seal it.

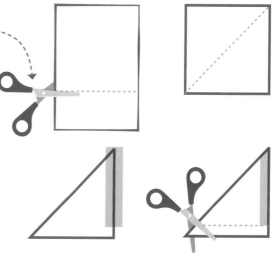

9. Now for the nose cone. Make a triangle of paper and fold a pointed corner around towards the centre point. Then fold the other point around the back until it comes full circle and meets the other points. Tape along the paper's edge.

10. Pop the cone over the end of the paper tube and make snips around the edge of the cone up to where it meets the rim of the tube, to create a snug fit. Tape the snipped paper to the paper tube.

11. Finally, tape the 3 fins onto the tube of the rocket.

Tip: make extra rockets around the left over pipe

Launch the rocket

12. Make sure the rocket can move freely up the launcher tube E, then push it into the angled elbow. Screw the pop bottle into the cap at the other end of the coupler, and put your launcher on the ground. Making sure no one is in the way, stamp really hard on the pop bottle, and your rocket will soar!

whoosh, watch your rocket go...

Super shrimp net

Shrimp are very tasty, and easy to catch at the seaside using a simple net. Now you can look forward to a shrimpy seafood snack!

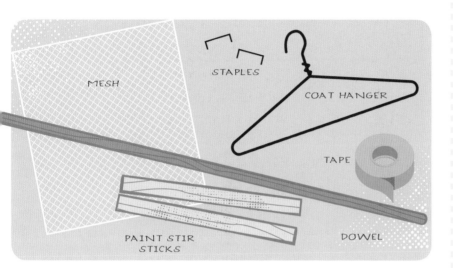

MESH

STAPLES

COAT HANGER

TAPE

PAINT STIR STICKS

DOWEL

you will need

- wire coat hanger
- 80cm sq fine white mesh netting
- paint stir sticks (x2)
- 2.5cm wood dowel, about 1m long
- hot glue/wood glue
- 15mm – 18mm industrial staples (x2)
- heavy-duty string (or floss)
- hacksaw
- pliers
- large needle
- tape
- ruler and pencil
- drill
- small drill bit
- hammer

1. Clip the top off a wire coat hanger with pliers.

2. Trim the paint stir sticks with a hacksaw to fit inside the coat hanger's bottom edge. Glue the sticks together. When dry, make a small notch with the hacksaw in the end of each stick.

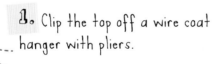

you may need help bending the wire...

3. Place the coat hanger in the middle of the sticks and bend the wire into the notches, then remove and set aside.

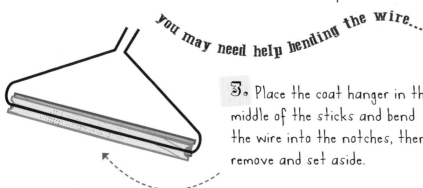

49

HOW TO FIND AND CATCH SHRIMP

Always consult a tide chart before shrimping, and keep an eye out for the incoming tide!

Late afternoon at low tide is the best time to catch shrimp, as the low tide will allow you to access deeper areas where shrimp gather, usually covered by the seawater.

Shrimp like to hang out in small bays that lead to the sea, or along piers and docks.

Try scraping your net along the beach and see what you find.

The shrimp may try to escape from your net while you are catching them, so use a sweeping motion to keep the shrimp in the net sock.

4. Next, centre the paint stir sticks on the dowel, glue in place and allow to dry completely.

Now for the net

5. Lay the mesh flat, fold it diagonally, then fold diagonally again. Using a few pieces of tape, stick the loose edges together at intervals to hold the net together. You now have your basic net shape - called a sock!

6. Cut a 1m length of floss and feed one end through the eye of the needle. Tie the ends of the floss together in a knot. Push the needle through the pointed end of the netting and loop it back through the floss to create a secure starting anchor.

7. Wrap the floss a couple of times around the edge of the netting and continue stitching along the edge, spacing your stitches about 1cm apart. Stop when you reach the end of the diagonal fold. Finish off with a knot.

8. Weave the wire hanger through the sock about 2cm from the edge, then sew the mesh netting around the hanger. Finally, carefully remove the tape.

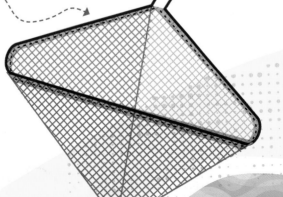

Time to assemble

9. Stand the dowel upright with the paint stir sticks facing upwards. Measure the width of the staple (make a note of it) and mark 2 sets of holes to this width on the paint stick over the dowel.

10. Drill 4 small holes, known as pilot holes, into the dowel. These holes should be smaller in diameter than the ends of the staples, and will prevent the wood from splitting when the staples are hammered home.

Take care!

you'll need help holding the dowel...

11. Now place the bent coat hanger with the mesh sock back onto the paint stir sticks and around the notches. Then carefully hammer the staples over the hanger and through the stir sticks, into the dowel below.

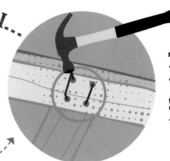

Tip: Hold the staple with pliers when you first tap it in, to hold it steady.

90°

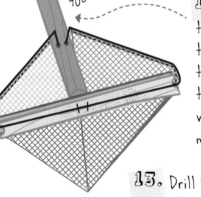

12. Bend the ends of the hanger back towards the dowel and use pliers to bend them at 90° to the dowel. Make a mark where the bent wire ends meet the dowel.

13. Drill 2 small openings at the pen marks partway through the dowel (not completely through). Glue the bent wire ends into the openings. Pull any loose mesh up towards the top of the wire triangle and cinch together with needle and floss. Now you're ready to go shrimping!

Simple spinning motor

you will need

- AA or AAA battery
- neodymium magnet (about same diameter as battery)
- 30cm stiff copper wire (or solid-core wire)
- scissors
- pliers
- pencil

You can make a very simple spinning motor with just a battery, a magnet, and some copper wire.

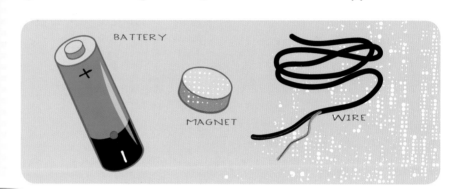

BATTERY

MAGNET

WIRE

✻ You may need help pulling the coating off the wire.

1. If the copper wire has a vinyl coating, remove it by gently squeezing a pair of scissors around the middle of the wire. Turn the wire slowly until you feel the scissors bite into the metal, but not cut through it. Slowly pull the vinyl coating off the wire. Repeat with the rest of the coating.

2. Using your fingers and pliers (be careful not to pinch your fingers), bend the wire in half and squeeze the wire to a point.

3. With the wire doubled over, curve it into a half-heart shape, then prise it apart so that it forms a full heart shape.

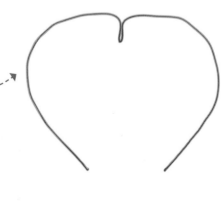

52

4. Put the battery on the flat (negative) end of the magnet so it fits snuggly, with the positive end pointing upwards.

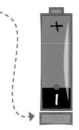

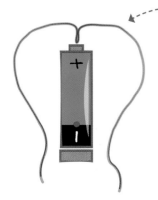

5. Place the bent wire over the battery so the point of the heart-shape touches the point of the battery. Bend the ends of the wire legs towards the base.

HOW THE MOTOR WORKS

A battery has a positive (+) and a negative (−) pole, and so does a magnet. By placing a magnet on the battery you provide an external magnetic field which causes the conductor (the wire) to turn when the circuit is complete. If the wire is in parallel with the magnetic field they share the same axis of rotation and will spin freely.

6. This next bit is tricky! Use pliers to bend the end of one wire 90° where the legs meet the magnet. Repeat this process with the other leg to make a pair of 'feet'.

✻ make a nice curve with the pliers

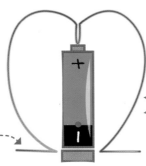

Take care!

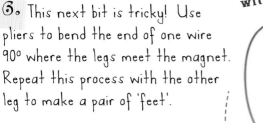

7. Bend one of the feet to form a half circle that will fit around the battery. Repeat with the other foot to form a circle. Trim the wire if it's too long.

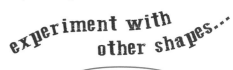
experiment with other shapes...

8. Set the battery on its end, on the magnet. Drop the wire frame on top of the battery and watch it spin! (Don't let it spin too long as it can get hot! Knock it off the battery with a pencil.)

Tip: You may need to tweak the wire for it to balance and let the motor spin without falling off the battery.

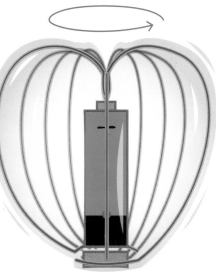

Super solar oven

Solar ovens require no electricity or fire, just direct sunlight, and are a great way to heat up a meal. Here's how to make a very inexpensive one. Afterwards, you could make a larger oven from wood in exactly the same way, giving you more reflected heat and a larger heating area.

you will need

- 2 cardboard boxes (one should fit inside the other, the smaller one should have a lid)
- aluminium foil
- glue
- glue brush
- black craft paper
- newspaper
- clear plastic

ALUMINIUM FOIL

LARGE CARDBOARD BOX

SMALL CARDBOARD BOX

CLEAR PLASTIC

GLUE

BLACK CRAFT PAPER

NEWSPAPER

Tip: Any two boxes that nest inside one another will work.

1. First, open the larger box and line the flaps with aluminium foil. Glue the foil to the flaps, making sure the foil's shiny side is facing upwards. (The reflective surface of the foil will direct the sun's rays onto your food and heat it up.)

2. Fold the flaps of the smaller box inwards and line it with black craft paper. (Black paper absorbs light, creating heat energy.) This box will be where you place your food.

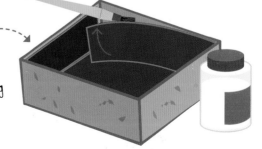

54

3. Crumple newspaper and place a layer in the bottom of the box with reflective flaps, then place the smaller matte black box inside the larger box. Stuff crumpled newspaper in the gap between the two boxes.

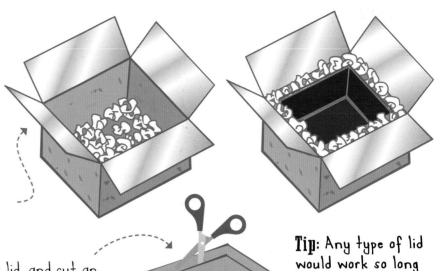

4. Next, take the small box lid, and cut an opening in it, leaving a border of about 20mm on all sides.

Tip: Any type of lid would work so long as it covers the inner box and has a windowed top.

5. Cover the opening with clear plastic. Rigid, clear plastic from a food container would work well, but so could plastic cling film. Tape the plastic to the underside of the box lid, then, place the lid on the matte black box.

6. Your solar oven is almost ready! First, position the oven so the flaps will reflect the sun directly into the centre chamber. Place your food in a heat-resistant dish (such as a stone plate or ceramic bowl) and wait. Depending on how much sun there is and how intense it is, your solar oven should start heating up. It's not uncommon for solar ovens to reach 120-150 C!

✻ Make sure your food is completely cooked before you eat it!

Go go go kart

Always wanted a go kart? Here's how to make one! This is a single-brake go cart for use on flat surfaces. It is quite a complicated project and will need lots of planning and organisation. The key is to prepare everything before you start putting it all together.

you will need

- 12.5mm plywood sheets
- 10x5cm timber
- drill + drill bits
- screws - various lengths
- coach bolt
- 10mm threaded metal rod (x2)
- spacers (x4)
- nuts + washers (to fit rod)
- 4 sturdy wheels
- bungee cable
- 1.5cm-thick natural fibre rope

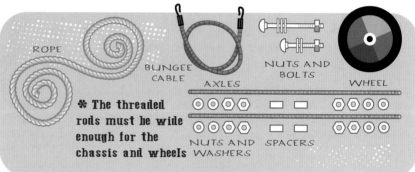

ROPE

BUNGEE CABLE

AXLES

NUTS AND BOLTS

WHEEL

✻ The threaded rods must be wide enough for the chassis and wheels

NUTS AND WASHERS

SPACERS

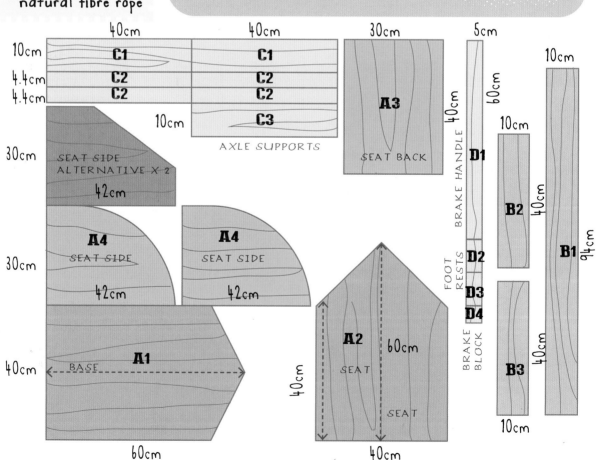

Making the seat and chassis

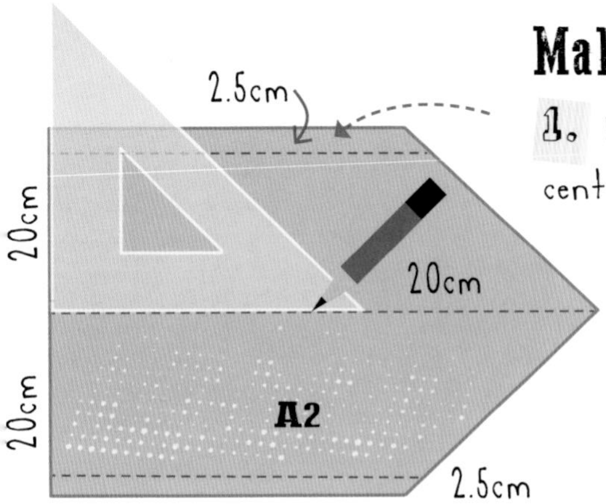

1. Using a ruler, measure in 20cm from the edge to find the centre of the seat. Then, using the set square, draw a centre line and extend it until you meet the end point.

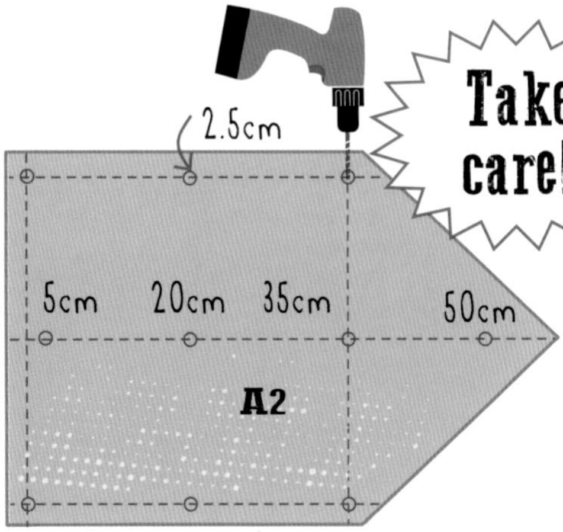

2.5cm

20cm

20cm

20cm

A2

2.5cm

2.5cm

Take care!

5cm   20cm   35cm   50cm

A2

2. Next, with a pen mark the base with a series of holes as shown on the diagram. Using an awl, make holes on the marks, then carefully drill pilot holes right through the base.

3. For the chassis, measure and draw 3 lines 2.5cm apart, along the length of the longest spar, then a series of lines at right angles as shown here. Mark a series of points, as shown, then drill the next pilot holes.

＊ Draw 2 lines at an angle then saw along these lines to make a point.

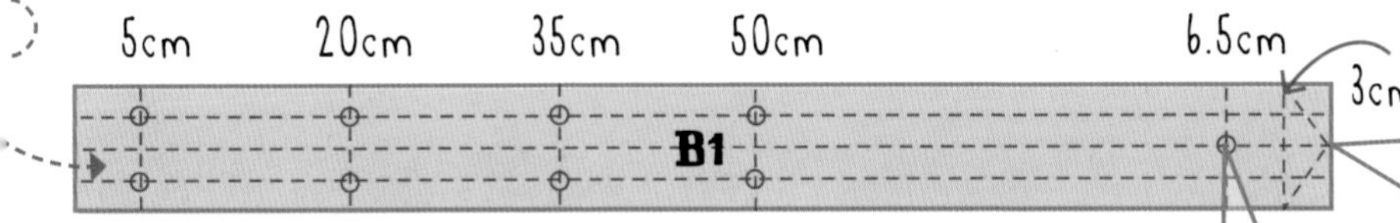

5cm   20cm   35cm   50cm   6.5cm

3cm

B1

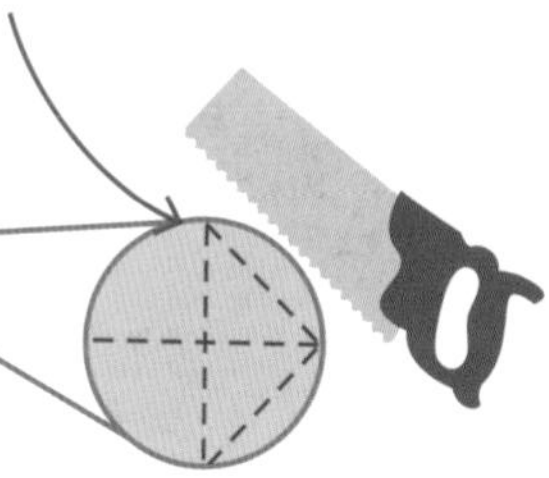

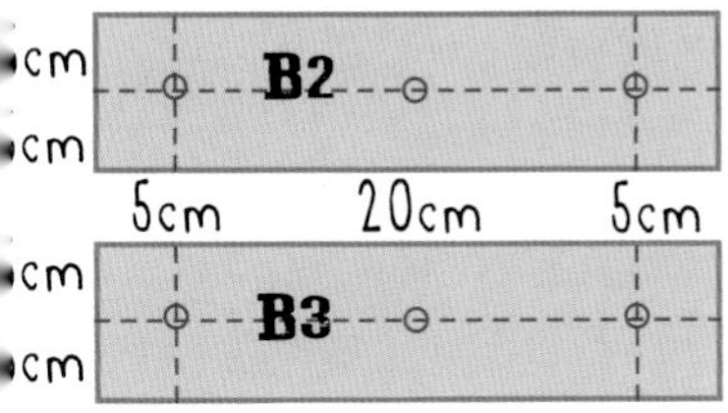

B2

5cm   20cm   5cm

B3

4. Measure and draw a line along the centre of the 2 smaller spars. Mark and drill 3 holes in each piece.

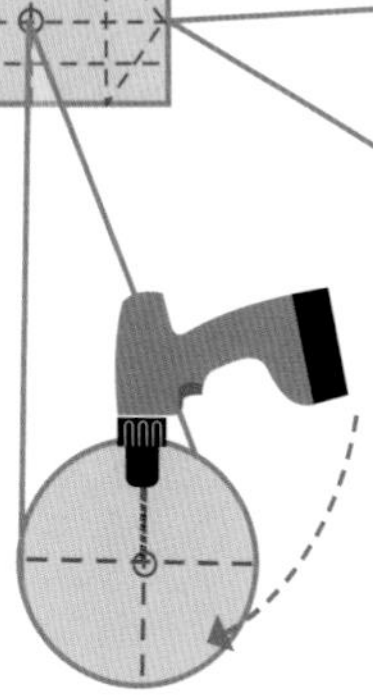

5. Using a large drill bit drill a hole 6.5cm from the end, big enough for the coach bolt to pass through.

6. Screw the 2 smaller spars to the outer edges of the base. Next, using the centre line as a guide, screw the main spar along the centre of the base.

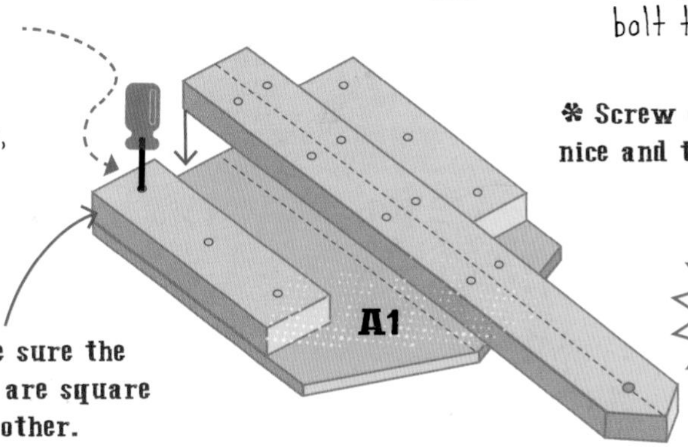

＊ Screw everything nice and tight.

Need a hand?

＊ Make sure the corners are square to each other.

A1

7. Position the seat on top of the chassis, and using an awl (or pen) mark the screw holes onto the spars below. Remove the seat then drill a short pilot hole into each mark.

Finally screw the seat in position, making sure the screw heads are embedded into the wood.

TIP

You could use a counter-sink drill bit to make slightly indented holes for the screw heads.

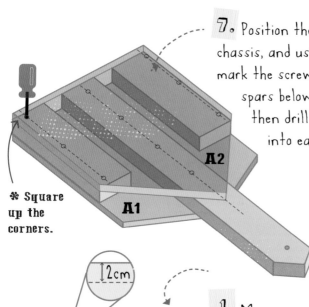

A2

A1

✻ Square up the corners.

12cm

6cm   34cm
C2
4cm   20cm   36cm

C2
4cm   20cm   36cm

1. Measure a line 2cm from the edge for both pieces, then mark the screw holes as shown.

Making the rear axle

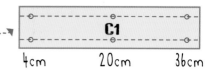

C1

4cm   20cm   36cm

2. Measure a line 2cm from the edge and mark screw holes as shown along both lines.

3. Drill pilot holes through the marks on all 3 pieces of wood.

time to assemble the axle

4. Turn the chassis up side down then screw the 5-holed C2 piece in place using the 6cm and 34cm holes.

Next slide one of the axle rods between the two pieces, then put the second C2 wood piece in place.

6cm

C1

34cm

C2   **C2**

✻ Important! Turn this support round the opposite way, so that the holes align with C1.

Need a hand?

TIP

Use G clamps to hold the wood in place.

5. Now place the C1 piece of wood on top and drop 6 screws into the holes. Make sure the pieces of wood are all aligned, and the rod can rotate easily.

6. Carefully screw the screws through to the base below, making sure everything is screwed down very tightly.

Making the seat back

1. Measure a line 12.5mm from the straight edges then make a mark for 4 screw holes as shown half-way between the line and the edge of the wood.

Now do the same along the bottom edge.

2. Repeat for the other side piece.

3. Measure a line 12.5mm from the straight edge, then make marks as shown between the edge and the line.

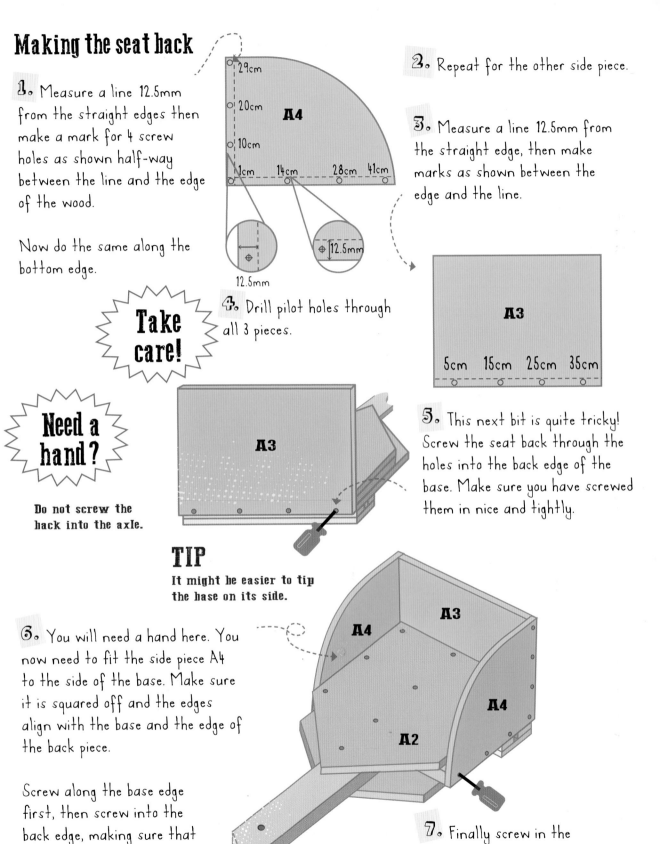

A4

29cm
20cm
10cm
1cm   14cm   28cm   41cm

12.5mm

12.5mm

A3

5cm   15cm   25cm   35cm

Take care!

4. Drill pilot holes through all 3 pieces.

Need a hand?

Do not screw the back into the axle.

A3

5. This next bit is quite tricky! Screw the seat back through the holes into the back edge of the base. Make sure you have screwed them in nice and tightly.

TIP

It might be easier to tip the base on its side.

6. You will need a hand here. You now need to fit the side piece A4 to the side of the base. Make sure it is squared off and the edges align with the base and the edge of the back piece.

Screw along the base edge first, then screw into the back edge, making sure that the edge is straight.

A4   **A3**

A4

A2

7. Finally screw in the other side panel.

Making the front axle

5cm 10cm   30cm 35cm

C3

3cm

❋ The hole is off centre so it won't collide with the axle rod.

2cm

D2

1. Draw a centre line along the foot block, and make 2 marks 2cm from each end for both blocks. Drill holes for the screws.

Take care!

2. Draw a line 2cm along both edges of the wider axle support, make a series of marks for the screws, then drill the holes.

3. Make a mark for the coach bolt, but don't drill a hole just yet!

5. Take axle support C1 and stack the C2 strips on top, sliding the axle rod in between. Top with the drilled support C3, then screw all 3 layers together, nice and tight.

C3

C1

C2

❋ Remove the axle rod when fixed together!

4. Draw a line 2cm from the edge, then make marks and drill holes to match C3.

5cm 10cm   30cm 35cm

C2

C2

6. With a 2cm drill bit drill a hole right the way through all 3 layers. Then drill another 2 holes 2cm from the corner for the rope.

Take care!

2cm

2cm

2cm

1cm

7. Screw the foot blocks onto the axle 1cm from the short edge as shown. Make sure they are fixed tightly.

❋ Add the axle rod!

8. Pop a washer on top of the main spar, and slide the coach bolt through the washer, spar, and front axle. Screw the nut onto the bottom of the bolt and screw tightly in postion.

❋ Add a second nut for extra security!

❋ Tighten the nuts against each other to lock them in place.

9. Finally add a washer, a spacer, a washer, a wheel, a washer, and 2 nuts onto each end of the axle rod. Phew! Remove any excess rod with a hacksaw.

Fitting the brake

Take care!

20cm

D1

30cm

1. Draw a line along the centre of the handle, then make a mark 20cm along from the end. Drill a hole. Turn the handle on its side and drill 2 small holes, 2cm apart.

2. Turn the cart on its side and make a mark on the seat side. Put a pen through the handle hole over the mark, to make sure the pivot point is about 15cm ahead of the axle placement.

15cm

A4

* You may need to adjust the hole position depending on the size of the wheels.

3. If you are happy with the pivot postion, drill a 1.5cm hole in the seat side for the bolt. Slide the bolt through the handle and side, and tighten the nuts.

D4

Need a hand?

4. Mark and drill 2 holes diagonally across the brake block. Screw in postion just above the brake lever, to keep the brake in place.

5. Put the bungee ends in the handle and using a pen, stretch it taut around and underneath the base of the cart. Make a mark with the pen.

6. Screw 2 holes either side of the mark and add 2 screws. Stretch the bungee back to fit around the screws. Make sure the ends fit tightly in the lever holes.

off you go...

Stay Safe!
Go carts can be dangerous. Do not ride your go cart down slopes!

7. Finally, slide the ends of the rope through the front axle holes and knot firmly underneath to the right length for you.

* Use your feet and rope to steer your cart.

Materials and where to find them

Materials you can find in a stationers or art & craft shop

You might already have these materials – they always come in handy for crafty projects:

- A4 paper
- marker pens
- paint
- paper clips
- PVA glue
- sticky tape
- thin card

Materials you can find in the supermarket

You're likely to have many of these materials in your kitchen and around the house. If not, you can buy them from a supermarket or online.

- AA batteries
- balloons
- candles
- cling film
- cocktail sticks
- guar gum (this can be hard to find in shops, but can be bought online)
- heavy-duty bin bags
- matches
- pool noodle (these can be hard to find in shops, but can be bought online)
- straws
- surgical spirit
- tinfoil

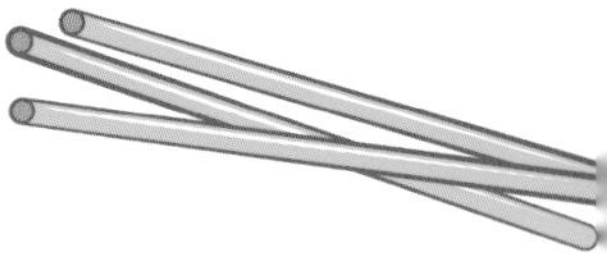

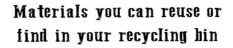

Materials you can find in a DIY store and garden centre

The staff in your local DIY shop should be able to help you find the correct materials and equipment for your project.

- 2 x 2 timber
- 2 x 4 timber
- copper wire
- duct tape
- exterior grade plywood
- eye bolt
- fine mesh netting
- gaffer tape
- industrial staples
- metal washers and bolts
- neodymium battery
- paint
- paint stir stick
- PVC 4-way connector
- PVC elbow
- PVC non-threaded coupler
- PVC pipe
- rope
- sandpaper
- seeds
- small plant pot
- thick string / twine
- weed barrier cloth
- wood glue
- wooden dowel

Materials you can reuse or find in your recycling bin

There are plenty of things you can make out of old junk and recyclables, instead of throwing them away. Here are materials needed for the projects in this book that you might already have:

- broom handle
- cardboard boxes
- coin cell battery and holder
- egg box
- hardcover book
- juice carton
- lint (this can be found in the tumble drier filter. An alternative material for making fire lighters is the fluffy paper material inside eco jiffy bags).
- mobile phone vibration motor
- old newspaper
- old toothbrush
- plastic bags
- plastic container with lid
- plastic liquid container
- plastic pop bottle
- wire coat hanger

Index